MAKING
DOLLARS
& SENSE WORK

MAKING DOLLARS
& SENSE WORK

A Financial Primer for
Single Moms & Dads
Plus College Kids, Too!

ROCHELLE CAMPBELL

Interior design and formatting by

www.emtippettsbookdesigns.com

MAKING DOLLARS & SENSE WORK

Table of Contents

Opening Thought:
Sailing Through Dreams

<u>SAILING THROUGH DREAMS</u>

Dreaming our dreams we often fail;
to dream big enough or, strong enough
for it to catch shape and sail.
We discover a wave and then we shudder.
We re-jigger, re-boot, re-think and stall.
We form half-dreams that lead to half-lives
in which we stumble and fall.
But, if we lift our thoughts, our voices, our eyes
we can aim for higher highs;
Then, and only then, we'll sail straight through our
dreams…
and land upon our new reality's shore.

~ Rochelle Campbell

Why I Wrote This Book

WHEN I WAS growing up I lived with my Mom in a three-bedroom apartment in Brooklyn, NY. She was a nurse and worked hard to make ends meet. She was a tough mother who wanted only the best for her only child — me.

Mom wanted me to be the best and brightest but she had a definite way she thought I should go about it. She also had a very precise manner in which she felt it best to "teach" me how to be the best me that she thought I could be.

My Mom showed by example that hard work, saving, rationing meals, cutting coupons, buying frugally, buying the no-frills brands, and staying off Ma Bell's beige rotary dial phone would slowly make us solvent.

But see, I didn't *get* that then. Back then, I thought my mother was a cheapskate. I thought she wanted me to suffer. I thought she wanted me to be ostracized by my peers in school for wearing last season's fashions. I did a whole lot of thinking but down some very different paths than those my mother thought along.

As I matured, some of the pieces of my mother's financial genius began to reveal themselves. As a single mother, she put me through private school for middle school to ensure I was well-prepared for high school and would get into a good one. I did her a solid by getting skipped a year saving her a ton of money. When I graduated from the 9th grade, I distinctly remember her telling me that she had gotten used to paying my school tuition. Instead of having more money to spend, she told me she wanted to put that money previously earmarked for my schooling to good use.

What did she do? She purchased a timeshare so that we would always have an inexpensive vacation each and every year.

My mother sat down each pay week with pen and paper and figured out her budget so that she could meet her goals.

I saw her doing this but never knew what her goals were. She never showed me what she was doing; she just told me the general idea that she was creating a budget so that there would be enough money for all the things we needed.

But, what were all the things we needed?! See, this is where her "teaching" did not mesh with how I prefer to learn. I like having all of the details there in front of me. I prefer to have things explained in detail, at least once, so that I can grasp the concept and ask any questions bugging my mind. Mom didn't do Q & A. Mom just did. She expected me to pick it up like she did.

What my mother failed to realize is that there are many different ways to learn and the way she learned was not the same way that I learned. It was a different generation; a different time. There were so many rules and standards to live by that kept her and previous generations safe. However, all those rules and mores were being turned on their head as I was growing up. By the time I was a teenager, the rulebook my mother grew up with was antiquated.

I wrote this book because the financial genius of my mother sat in my subconscious mind and inspired me throughout the years to do better, and be better, with my life and my money. It took me years to bring that inner financial potential into my life. I had to read many books, talk to a lot of people, ask questions of my more fiscally responsible friends and listen to what they said — really listen to gain a firm understanding of what my mother seemed to intuit effortlessly. She understood that putting yourself and your savings *first* is of utmost importance; that timely bill payments and sensible spending as you put away a third, or more, of your yearly income is truly the way to financial freedom.

I wrote this book so that people who need to see concrete examples of how the basics of a family's financial structuring is done can get what they need when they need it which is *now.*

You've probably read a lot of material yourself in books, magazines, or online about how to be a great Mom, or Dad. Or, what it takes to be a successful young person starting out in life. So why should you read this book? A book geared to parents and college-aged folks about finances. What could a book about finances possibly help you with your family and their challenges? Because by having a solid financial base for one's family you open yourself and your loved ones to opportunities that you may not have had access to, or could capitalize on. By having a firm handle on your finances, you can make decisions fairly quickly and re-allocate monies within a pay cycle, or two, if need be.

This book is not for a particular age group. It is geared for single parents and college kids to help us get the basics of finances under our belts, or to remind us what's most important so we can get back on the bandwagon.

Who am I — other than my mother's child? I've been a single mother for the past 14 years. However, I was married for nine years prior to my single mother days. So, I've seen finances on both sides of the parent fence – the single side and the married side. I have found that both states of being have their challenges and benefits. The most obvious, and pertinent to this book's focus, is the additional income of a two-income home.

Yet, even those of us who are currently married will find helpful techniques in this book that can help their family, or as mentioned above, the steps laid out in this book will serve as a reminder for what you already know but may be too busy to put into full effective *consistent* practice in your family.

Lastly, now that I have a college-aged son I wanted to make sure that I imparted clear, concise steps to help him have a solid financial start in life.

The underlying theme of this book revolves around how a family's finances affect the decisions, choices, and, in some cases, the opportunities available to one's family. By expanding your financial know-how, you expand your opportunities. This book is simple and straightforward and provides an overview of the specific pieces of your financial life that can be improved right now as well as pieces that need more nurturing.

Making Dollars & Sense Work is a collection of things that I have learned that have worked for me and my family and may work for you and yours. This will be a short book. Why? Because we're busy folks! We have things to do and we don't have a whole lot of time to do them. We have hopes, dreams, and children to raise. We have goals and people to meet. We don't have time to waste.

Without further ado...

CHAPTER 1:
When the Children Want Things You Can't Afford

THIS WAS MY biggest and worst nightmare *ever*. I have two sons and a little girl. My boys came first and are now 18 and 15 while my daughter is 17 months old. (Yeah, I am a bit nuts.)

My biggest fear prior to having children: *How was I going to be able to afford college?* When my oldest son became nine, he wanted piano lessons, followed by guitar lessons, archery, and a host of toys with price tags that made me blink in rapid succession.

At that time, I was earning barely over $30,000 and lived in the expensive urban jungle of Brooklyn, NY where rent in a decent neighborhood was over the recommended 25 – 35% of one's net income (the amount of money you actually bring home).

I was not the sharpest tool in the shed at that point in my life because I had tunnel vision. I was focused on making my children's life happy, exciting and idyllic to the best of my ability. I made choices almost 20 years ago that I'm not sure if I would ever do again. In fact, the choices I made then are *still* affecting me today. However, some of what I did right, back then is, as follows:

Search for the item your child wants, or a similar item online

Everyone knows this, right? But have you searched the online shopping networks such as QVC, EVINE Live (formerly Shop HQ), HSN, JTV, etc.? These shopping networks help you to stretch your dollar because many of them can be cheaper than what you can find in the stores AND they offer attractive payment methods.

Each network calls it something different but the idea is that they break up your payment over 3 – 6 installments on your credit, or debit card. Yet, they ship the item to you after you pay your first installment which will include your shipping charge. Then, the other installments will be billed every 30 days until you pay it off. There is no additional charge, or fee, for this awesome service but it does help with cash flow. It will stretch your payments out over time, which we usually have more of than money!

Sometimes you can even get designer items on these convenient stretch-pays, or easy-pays which make you the Superstar Mom, or Dad, without breaking the bank. A word of advice — make sure you can afford the combined payments of multiple items ordered on these flexible terms. If you order 10 items and the payment is $15 each that is $150 a month for 3 – 4 months — can your budget handle that?

Music, Sports and Other Lessons on the Cheap

When my son wanted piano lessons, I nearly freaked out. Those lessons are expensive! That is, until a very close friend of mine suggested that I seek out a music school college student who could use extra cash. Call your local college, or university, and ask to speak with the Student Affairs Office, the person in charge of the Student Center, or the job board person of that school's newspaper, or radio station. Once you get that person, let them know why you're calling and see if they can help you, or direct you to someone who can. It may take a few phone calls (or, 6 or 7...) but it will be worth it. Anything that is worth it takes time to procure.

You can secure tutors for specific subject areas using the same technique. Instead of calling the above departments, call the specific department that your child needs tutoring. If it's math, call the Mathematics department and speak to the Director, or their assistant. If your child needs assistance in biology, call the Biology department head, etc. (This tip came from my editor!)

Here's one more – hire a college or high school student to tutor children in lower grades. Make sure you pay at least minimum wage per hour (as of 12/31/14 the minimum wage in New York is $8.75/hour; as of 7/1/14 it is $9/hour in California; as of 1/1/14 it is $7.25 in Texas; etc.). However, $10 – 25 per hour would be preferable, depending upon your budget. This is decidedly cheaper than the professional piano teacher which can be $50 – 125 per lesson.

The idea of seeking a person in training (who has been in training for 2-3 years) is a valid one for all types of activities. If your child is interested in something else like knitting, or crocheting, then seek someone who is older (retired) who may be seeking additional income and possibly, company.

Your child's interests will guide you on where to look for your semi-professional that you can easily afford.

Weekend Activities That Won't Break the Bank

The weekend's coming. What to do? Chuck E. Cheese? Too darned expensive? Got you! I used to go to the Cheese guy's place when I received those lovely email coupons for extra coins and the meal deals. That was the only time I went! This way, $30 – 40 would ensure a solid 2-3 hour play and eating time that my sons could enjoy and I could rest a bit while watching them run around and play.

When that was too much money I put my research skills to work and sought out local activities that would be of interest to my sons. In my area, I found a nature center that hosted regular free workshops. It was in a large park near my home and they offered bird watching tours, canoeing, arts and crafts, where they made picture frames from natural materials gathered in the park, etc. I found free archery and chess classes (still had to buy the bow, arrows and fund the trips related to these activities…). We went to numerous free festivals during the summer and enjoyed movies in the park, or on the beach.

Depending upon where you live, you can find tons of things that may interest your child(ren). Nonprofit organizations are the BEST! If they don't offer programs directly for children many times they can direct you to programs that may be of interest to your children.

Yes, you have to dig and research but that is FREE. Do it when they're sleeping and then when they're awake and you go, you're again — Superstar Mom, or Dad! You can even invite their friends along and make it even more special for everyone.

You can literally type into your favorite search engine — *free activities for boys/girls in (your city, state)* and see what pops up. If there are specific activities you're seeking put the name of the activity in there, too. You will get lists, websites, specific programs, and the like. Now, you have to sort through, read and dig among the many results to see what's there and what may be of interest to your children.

Don't forget the easy things like the Y, PAL (Police

Athletic League), Boys' Clubs, Boy Scouts, Girl Scouts, sports teams organized by local businesses, or companies that may offer free or low-cost uniforms.

Did I mention I found a pottery workshop in a park with a working kiln in a neighborhood where I lived when the boys were younger? The whole family filled molds with Plaster of Paris, painted our pieces and left them to be fired by the workshop coordinator — all for free!

Sometimes, you just have to walk around and ask people if they know of cool things to do with kids. The worst they can tell you is they don't know of anything. The best? They know of something, or they can direct you to someone who does know of great activities.

Another tip from my editor is to check into volunteer activities. She shared with me that with her New Jersey horseback riding center, the teens earned time learning to ride a horse, once they did their volunteer hours. That particular riding center even had a monthly program for younger kids. Check out groups, nonprofits and other organizations in your area. Some of them may have a program that may interest your child(ren) and may include learning a skill that will serve them long after they leave childhood.

The goal here is to keep your children busy so they cannot get into anything unsavory.

One Very Big DON'T

If you're feeling the pinch for cash because your child(ren) want something, or want to go somewhere do not take out a pay day loan. This is the absolute worst thing you can do to yourself unless you have an IRON WILL.

A pay day loan's interest rate ranges from 457% - 1,369% depending upon when you pay back the loan. No, the above rates are not typos. Read the fine print of the payday loan contracts. The fees are very, very expensive.

If you take out a $250 loan and you pay it off on your next pay day you will pay them back $325. That's a $75 fee for floating your money for 7 – 14 days, or 30%. In a pinch not too bad, right? Wrong. That's $75 you will never see again that could pay a bill, put into savings, or do something meaningful for your kids.

The real problem is the pay down option that *most* people choose instead of paying off the loan in full the following pay week. These pay day companies offer you time to pay off your $250 loan. They offer a payment plan where you pay a portion of the principal and a set interest fee every pay week until you pay off the full principal of the loan.

To be precise: if you choose the pay down option on the $250 loan and you pay off $50 of your loan a week you will pay a fee of about $45 a pay week. So, the total owed to the payday company per pay week is $95 until you pay off the loan!

It will take you 5 pay weeks to pay off this $250 loan since you are only paying $50 towards the principal balance (this is the actual amount of money that you borrowed). The $45 fee every pay week is, in essence, the interest rate. By the end of this 5-pay week loan you will have paid this company $225 in interest in addition to the money you borrowed. In this example, you are paying almost double what you borrowed. Sounds suspiciously like loan sharking doesn't it? Well, it is. New York State's government calls it usury.

If you happen to be caught in a payday hell go to my website http://rochelleauthor.com/, click on the book's name in the upper right hand corner and enter the password: Free_Superstar_Docs to download the letter that will make the payday loan companies stop their vicious cycle. [Please note: this letter is for New

York State residents. However, most states have similar stances on this topic. Please refer to the appendix for web links to various states' official sites regarding payday loans.]

What these online payday loan companies are doing is illegal in most states as they are charging fees that are astronomical (way over 100% interest). Why do you think the guys that break kneecaps are not legal? For the same reason – the fees are too high for normal people to pay.

So, money that you could be using to pay for other things will get sucked into repaying a very small debt that will not go away. This scenario gets worse if you decided to take out more than one pay day loan at a time. You will need help because repaying two or more pay day loans is a debt that will suck your bank account dry!

A main goal of this book is to give single parents and college kids information that they may not have possessed before reading this book. This way, we can make more informed choices about our financial transactions.

When a single mom, or dad, is stressed their children, co-workers, friends and family are stressed. The stress does not remain in the home, or in a single parent's head. It is exuded almost through the pores. By shedding light on tough subjects and doing small things to begin addressing the large problem, things get better. Trust me — they do. But you have to keep at it knowing that your children are watching you. They are seeing how you live life and watch if you will do what you say you are going to do.

If you don't keep your promises to yourself, and to them, what hope do you have that they will keep their promises to themselves and others as they mature into adults? As parents, we have been entrusted to raise the next generation. What will that generation be like if we don't give it our all?

On an upbeat note, as your children get older and their wants become larger, it is my sincere hope that your income will also increase to match the growing demands. If not, you can look into crowd funding as a means of raising money for the thing(s) your child wants. One crowd funding platform that is great is <u>IndieGoGo</u>. This particular platform allows you to keep all monies raised even if you don't reach your stated financial goal. You pay a higher fee if you don't meet the goal but you do get to keep the monies raised. With other platforms, such as <u>Kickstarter</u>, if you don't meet your stated financial goal all monies raised in that campaign will be returned to the donors.

If you choose to go the crowd funding route, you will need social media savvy so you can spread the word about your child's fundraising campaign. You will also have to tap into groups, organizations, and people that have an affinity for the thing your child is interested in doing.

To back up a little, crowd funding is when a lot of people give a little bit of money (as little as $1 to 5) until the financial goal you've selected is met. You can even have individual donors that give $1,000, or more. It all depends upon the effectiveness of your campaign. So, it helps to ask friends and family for their input on the wording you choose, and the video you upload that will be available to all who view your child's crowd funding campaign.

You can use crowd funding for anything. Say your child is interested in going to summer camp for swimming. Let's say it is $1,700 for one week of camp and it will cost $100 for the roundtrip ticket to get your child to and from the camp. You will need $1,800 but you need to ask for $1,900 - $2,000 because there is a fee to use these crowd funding services. They charge 4.5 – 9% in order for you to post your campaign. If you ask for the exact amount you need for your child's trip you are basically saying that you will pay the crowd funding platform's fee out of your own pocket ——which you can choose to do. It's up to you and your budget.

There are always options out there. These are some ideas to get you thinking about ways to make things happen for your kids. My family used to do 50/50 potlucks if there was something that a member of the family needed. Everyone puts some money in a bag, or a box. At the end of the evening, the money is split between the person who wins and the person who is in need of the help and assistance. This way, one other person at the event feels like a winner, too.

The only thing limiting us single parents is our imagination on how we can make things happen for the benefit of our kids.

All of this leads us to a topic I know many of us don't want to deal with — our personal finances.

CHAPTER 2:
How Being a Great Steward of the Coffers Makes You an A-1 Mom, or Dad

OKAY, I KNOW this is a nutty way to look at things especially when you live paycheck-to-paycheck but I have learned (the hard way!) that it is truly important.

The first thing that I would implement if I could go back in time: my one-page master finance spreadsheet. Over the last few years I created a spreadsheet to help me keep track of all of my bills, expenses and income — just one page!

I did not want a huge program that needed hours and hours of maintenance (like Quicken...). I tried several programs over the years and due to either laziness, or complexity I didn't like them and didn't stick to them. However, this one pager helps keep me on track with *no issues*.

In the upper right hand corner I enter all of my income so this way I know exactly how much money I bring in each month, from what source and on what date (or frequency). Once I get a total number, then I can build out the left side of the page.

On the left in the upper portion of the spreadsheet is where I detail the household living expenses such as rent, light, childcare expenses, gas, cable, cell phone, etc. The items that are germane to our shelter and quality of life. Then, under those, I add the other things such as any Netflix, or other automatic payments that I may have. I also put in this section my *savings*. Yes, I put savings in the mandatory section. Then, I total up all of these expenses.

The bottom section on the left is for the other things that change on a monthly basis — groceries, laundry, toiletries/household items, children activities, etc. Then, I total all of these expenses up.

Next to all of these items I put the date that each one is due in addition to how much is due. I will explain why later.

The trick becomes making the total of these two sections be LESS than your total net income each month. *That's* where the creativity on your part comes out. For many of us, these expenses are not less than what we make; it's more. So, how do you make it work? Can you make payment arrangements? Can you reduce a bill (or, two, or three)? Can you see if you can find a friend to share costs with so that certain bills can be halved? Can you barter to bring down your overall living costs?

Once you look at these things, you can then also look at increasing your income. Many times, this can include going back to school which will ultimately raise your bills, but the increase in income could possibly offset the increase in expenses. Only you can determine that fine point.

To help you with this, you can check online and find out if your local city government offers free financial counseling. In New York City, can call 311 and ask for an appointment for financial counseling and be given a phone number where you can meet with a financial counselor for FREE. It is usually facilitated by a local nonprofit organization. Here's the link for the Department of Consumer Affairs Office of Financial Empowerment — http://www.nyc.gov/html/ofe/html/find/find.shtml.

(That's a mouthful…)

If you'd like to get a template of this one-page Master Finances spreadsheet you can download it for free on my website. Simply go to http://rochelleauthor.com/, click on the tab with the *Making Dollars & Sense Work* book name in the top right hand corner and enter the password: Free_Superstar_Docs.

Once you have made this one-pager master finances sheet balance then all you need to do is pay each line item on the left every single month ON TIME. No, I don't mean to shout. This is just an emphasis that is very important.

Why? On to the next chapter!

Useful Search Strings

When looking for activities, after-school programs, pre-school, Headstart, or for anything for your children, try some of the search strings below, or some variation using your favorite search engine.

Please note, I prefer using Google as my search engine. I find it collects a very targeted set of results without extraneous links. Bing.com is my second favorite search engine.

SEARCH TIP: If you want to receive results that are very specific, meaning only what you type in, then put quotation marks around the search term(s) you want to ensure are in your search. You will generally receive fewer results but they will be much more specific.

For example, if you type into the Bing search engine, "free activities for kids in Arizona" you will receive 6 results.

If you use the same search string without the quotation marks you will receive 44,300,000 results. The power of quotation marks is truly amazing!

Okay, keeping the above in mind, play with using quotation marks in your searches to make your research go by a bit more quickly!

Free low cost childcare in (Your City, State)
Fun activities to do with kids (Your City, State)
After-school programs in (Your City, State)
Non-profit organizations kids' enrichment programs (Your City, State)
Creativity classes for kids (Your City, State)
Sports clubs for girls/boys

Swim team for tweens
Bowling for teens
Creative after-school programs for kids/tweens/teens/toddlers
Entrepreneurial boys/girls clubs or groups in (Your City, State)
Affordable childcare in (Your City, State)
Free fun activities in parks in (Your City, State)
[Enter your child's favorite activity/hobby] free in (Your City, State)

This is just a sampling of search strings that may be of assistance to you to get your research juices flowing. The idea here is that anything that you need can be available quickly with a few clicks on your keyboard. Yes, you may need to use different words/terms and drill down into pages 4, 5, 15, or 20 of the search to find that gem of a find that is *just right* for you and your family. However, no matter how long it takes it will be a benefit for you and your child(ren) once you secure that activity they love.

Something else to point out, you know your neighborhood, or area, best. You know the lingo for things in your neck of the woods. Use your insider's knowledge of your town to find activities, resources and programs for yourself and your children. Ask people you know if they have heard of anything. Reach out to your assembly person, your congressman and your senator to ask for any resources they can provide, or share. If you don't know who your elected officials are here is a link to help you identify them from Citizen Action Program Interactive: https://www.bipac.net/lookup.asp?g=bp. This link is for everyone to use in the United States. It will give you all of your local, state and federal elected officials.

Here are some additional links to resources in other states that may be of assistance to you.

CALIFORNIA

Free Tutoring Programs by City:
http://dcfs.lacounty.gov/edu/freetutoring/tutoringbycity.html

Torrance After-School Clubs:
https://www.torranceca.gov/Parks/7128.htm

*Free and Cheap After-School Classes and Programs
for LA Kids:*
http://la.mommypoppins.com/lakids/free-and-cheap-after-school-
classes-and-programs-for-la-kids\

*Free/Inexpensive Activities to Do at Home (sponsored by
First 5 California but anyone in any state can use!):*
http://www.first5california.com/parents/activity-center.aspx?id=16

CHSC Childcare Assistance Program:
http://www.chs-ca.org/child-care/ccap/

LOUISIANA

Free things to Do with Kids in New Orleans:
http://www.neworleanskids.com/freestuff.html

50 Free Things to Do in New Orleans:
http://www.neworleansonline.com/neworleans/attractions/
fiftyfreethings.html

MARYLAND

Approved Credit Counseling Agencies:
http://www.justice.gov/ust/eo/bapcpa/ccde/CC_Files/CC_
Approved_Agencies_HTML/cc_maryland/cc_maryland.htm

Find Quality Childcare:
http://www.marylandfamilynetwork.org/about/

*Child Care Subsidy Vouchers (state run maximum salary for
a family of 4 = $35,702):*
http://msde.maryland.gov/MSDE/divisions/child_care/
subsidy/#how

18

Y of Central Maryland (after-school programs, head start, enrichment programs, etc.)
http://ymaryland.org/programs/beforeafterschoolenrichment/beforeafterschool

NEW YORK

Fresh Air Fund (summer program for kids for low-income New Yorkers):
http://www.freshair.org/

TEXAS

Texas Outside:
http://www.texasoutside.com/texas-kids-activities/

50 Free Things to Do in Dallas, Texas:
http://www.tourtexas.com/content.cfm?id=136

Things to Do on a Budget on Galveston Island:
http://www.galveston.com/budgettravel/

Texas Association for the Gifted & Talented: Fun Things to Do (both online and outside the home):
http://txgifted.org/fun-things-do/
• Many of the links on this page can be utilized by anyone in any state! Check it out. •

YMCA of Austin - Low Cost Childcare & After-School Programs (plus a lot of other great programs!):
http://www.austinymca.org/programs/afterschool-care

AVAILABLE IN SEVERAL STATES

Youth Filmmaking Opportunities (for Teens):

19

http://www.pbs.org/pov/filmmakers/youth-filmmaking-programs.php#.VOQGXiz2TCN

Free Tutoring Under the 'No Child Left Behind' Law:
http://www.greatschools.org/students/homework-help/123-free-tutoring-no-child-left-behind.gs

Mommy Poppins is a great site that offers activities, after-school programs, tutoring and more in several metropolitan areas across the country including: New York City, New Jersey, Long Island, Connecticut, Westchester, Philadelphia, Boston and Los Angeles. You can begin exploring the site which spans all age groups, from babies to tweens, by clicking the link below. Then, click through to your desired metro area of interest.

http://boston.mommypoppins.com/

While I could research and share even more links that I find online the best thing I can do for you is to share with you search strings that you can use to find what you need when you need it. The links that I provide are valid and current today when I am writing this book in February/March 2015. However, if you pick this book up in 2017 these links may no longer work, or the programs could become defunct.

By sharing some ideas above about how I search for things, you can do your own 'fresh' searches whenever you want no matter in what year you pick this book up.

CHAPTER 3:
Why a Number Close to 800 is Your Best Friend -- Your Credit Report

I<small>T'S NOT JUST</small> single parents that have a hard time figuring out why they should care about their credit score. This is a topic that needs to be broadcast to all Americans as soon as they are mature enough to digest the information. Ahem, college students, wake up now. This is especially important for you!A lot of people are in the dark about the intricacies of understanding one's credit report and how to positively impact it. Yes, we can actually help our credit scores – or, begin building our credit scores — in very specific ways that are <u>not</u> intuitive.

If you're not signed up with Credit Karma (CK) do it yesterday! This handy FREE website that truly does not ever ask for a credit card will help you to get the upper hand on your financial life. Once you enroll, you will need to put your personal information in so that they can find *your* specific credit profile.

Once that's done, you can update your credit score every two weeks. They will even send you an email to let you know it's time to log in and update your credit score.

Now, comes the good part. Credit Karma breaks down your credit report to make it easier for you to get a handle on each aspect of your credit and shows you how each piece impacts your credit score.

For example, there are six categories that factor into your credit score:

Credit Card Utilization

Very simply your total credit card balances need to be below 50% of your total credit limit, or else you will get dinged in this category and your score goes down. It's best if your total credit card balances are no more than 20% of your total credit limit.

Specifically, let's say your total credit limit over 2 cards is $1,000 (keeping it simple folks!). That means that for each of your two cards your balance should not be more than <u>$100 on each card</u>. Yeah, so why bother having a credit card? That's beside the point. This is how your credit score is calculated. To get the <u>"A"ranking</u>, your credit card utilization should be between 1 – 20%.

Payment History

This is also a very simple one — pay your credit cards and all items listed on your credit report early, at the very latest on the day it is due. Some of your creditors may give you between 1 – 4 days of grace but this is not standard. You must communicate with EACH of your creditors to know if this is the case and which ones will grant you a grace period.

The best practice is to assume there is no grace period and pay your bill a couple of days early to ensure that no computer glitches/foul-ups affect the date your payment posts. (Yeah, you're dinged if *they* make a mistake and post later than you paid. It would then be your responsibility to follow-up with them and correct the error and have it removed from your credit report.)

If you miss a payment, it goes down on your credit report in the next billing cycle (usually 30/31 days later) and will remain on your credit report for up to 7 years. Yes, one missed payment can stain your report and lower your score tremendously! Needless to say, to get the *"A" ranking* you need to pay every single bill on time — 100% on time.

Derogatory Marks

This is the not so fun one. This is the area that messes up a lot of people simply because you are not informed when derogatory/negative information is added to your credit report. At least, not in an official manner. Derogatory marks are items that you did not pay through collection agencies, doctor/hospital bills that then go to a lawyer's office (read: collection agency) for payment. This category will also include defaulted student loans, car loans gone bad or any outstanding debt that a creditor wants to report. Of course, a bankruptcy goes in this section.

Negative information can remain on your credit report for up to 10 years. The credit reporting agency can take it off after 7 years but don't hold your breath. The "A" ranking is for having ZERO derogatory marks. [Please note: You will have a very difficult time getting a mortgage if you have derogatory marks. If you do have any, you will pay through most of your bodily orifices to get that house/condo/co-op loan.]

Age of Credit History

There's not much you can do about this category. The longer you've had credit the better your score. Only time will help you in this category. The "A" ranking is reserved for those accounts which you have held for 8 years, or longer.

Total Accounts

This category infuriates me. Why? To receive an *"A"*

ranking in this category you must have at least 22 credit accounts during the history of your credit file. So, here again, only time will help you on this factor. But here's the thing, if you wanted to try and get into the higher rankings for this factor you would have to open a number of accounts around the same time and then pay them on time each and every month for the life of that account (Yes, you can pay the minimum but you know the story with that! That needs an entire chapter unto itself to discuss!)

Credit Inquiries

This category details how many times a creditor has publicly reviewed (looked) at your credit report in order to see if they want to offer you credit. This can be done at your request, or if there are third-party creditors out seeking business they can pull your credit *without* your consent. Whether you have given consent, or not, your credit score goes down with EACH credit inquiry listed on your report.

Hard credit inquiries remain on your credit report for 2 years. That begs the question as to what a soft credit inquiry is, right? From my understanding, a soft credit inquiry is when an existing creditor checks your report on an existing line credit in order to decide if they want to give you an increase in credit limit. A soft inquiry can also be you requesting to look at your own credit report (when you ask one of the three reporting agencies for it.)

This usually is something offered to you after you have been denied credit. Funny. That's usually when you find out you have a problem! To get the "A" ranking in this category you must have ZERO credit inquiries. For the "B" ranking the number of credit inquiries is 1 – 2. [Now you see why category number 5 irritates me! In order to increase the number of total accounts, you will incur credit inquiries. Therefore, your score will decrease with each credit pull to (ha, ha) increase your credit score.]

Okay, I'll stop ranting.

As you can see, there are a number of things that we collectively need to know about our credit reports that we did not know. No one told us. Heck, most people are not told. We find out by trial and error, or we decide to teach ourselves because we're sick and tired of being sick and tired. Maybe that's why you're reading this book...because you want to find a key to help you unlock the next better section of your life. A life that you can share abundance with your children, with your other loved ones...with yourself.

One last note, <u>Credit Karma</u> has very recently upgraded their website. You can now login for *free* and acquire two of the three credit reporting bureau scores — Trans Union and Equifax! No more having to pay $10 – 30 just for your credit score, or go and apply for credit and ask what your score is. So, with a soft inquiry (no detriment to your credit score), Credit Karma has helped you yet again. [If you haven't signed up with Credit Karma yet — go do it now. I'll wait... you still here??]

CHAPTER 4:
"Innocent" Credit Report Zap -- Don't Let This Happen to You

BIG AREA THAT bugged me to no end after I came into financial stewardship awareness is the blatant disregard department stores have for you and your credit report. What do I mean by this? Let me ask you a question. The last few times you've gone to your favorite department store, electronics store, big box retailer, or your favorite online vendor, did they inquire if you'd like to apply for their credit card?

Come on, admit it. They did.

Remember what we just learned in Chapter 3. Every time you apply for credit your credit score is lowered. Now, depending upon the specifics of your particular credit report, a few hard credit inquiries may not hurt you. However, if you are in a precarious credit score position with a score in the mid-500s, or early 600s the willy-nilly addition of hard credit inquiries is *not* something you want to do.

Say, for instance, that for your birthday, or for some special occasion, you decided to go on a shopping spree. You planned out this shopping excursion with your one-pager firmly uppermost in your mind and you *know* you can afford to spend a very specific dollar amount.

However, you stop at five different stores and at each one the cashier asks you if you'd like to get 10 – 25% off of your purchase today. You, of course, say, *Sure!* And they proceed by asking your social number and other key information needed for a credit check.

Whoa! It is a bit of a bait-and-switch deal. Many stores just simply ask you directly if you'd like to apply for their credit card. A few will endeavor to gain more yes's by engaging in this slightly manipulative behavior. It is up to you to stop the cashier, or store employee, immediately and get more information from them before you move forward.

This would entail you having up-to-date information about your credit score/credit standing. This comes from monitoring your credit report even after you've ensured that it is as good and clean as you can get it.

Once you know your score, and specifically, how many hard inquiries are currently on your reports, the number of accounts you have open, and what your credit card utilization currently is, you can make an informed decision if applying for a credit card would be a good action for you to take.

For example, if you are looking to build your credit, it is a great idea to apply strategically for credit. As a young person starting out, apply to no more than two credit card companies a year. While it generally takes up to 2 years for a hard credit inquiry to be removed from your credit report, I have been told by people with good credit (scores higher than 700) that a hard credit inquiry comes off of their credit reports after 6 – 7 months.

Even if this is truly the case, don't get too happy and go applying all over town for things. Remember, to get an "A" ranking in the credit inquires department the credit reporting bureaus are looking for *zero* inquiries. So, be very mindful of how many inquiries are on your report and when they are scheduled to drop off. As another added benefit, Credit Karma does tell you when each inquiry is scheduled to be removed from your report.

To wrap this section up, I will tell you how much fun I have with cashiers and department store clerks when they try to entice me to apply for their store's credit card. I ask them directly if this would entail a hard inquiry to my credit report. This question usually stops them in their tracks. They look at you and blink a few times. The better ones call their manager immediately.

Then, the doe-eyed ones who are just following their supervisor's orders begin to try and steer you away from your question by telling you about the huge store discount you will receive if you apply — and get approved — today. All the while, dodging your questions about interest rates, if there is an annual fee, and is the rate variable or fixed. (Yeah, you should ask them these questions to know if that card will cost you money for having it in your wallet.)

In fact, the lower the interest rate on this proposed credit card the better. You should look for an interest rate of 15%, or less. If you know your credit score is low, your interest rate will automatically jump to over 20%; sometimes for people with a credit score lower than 620, the offered interest rates can be as high as 29.99%. Ouch!

For example, if you had a credit card with a $1,000 balance and a 15% interest rate, you would pay $150.00 to your creditor in fees. If you had a 29.99% interest rate on the same $1,000 credit balance, you would pay $299.00 — double the 15% interest rate. Interest is another name for the money credit card companies, and other retailers, charge you for using their money. So, finding the lowest interest rate is in your best interest!

On top of the high rate, there may also be an annual fee of $40 just for being a cardholder. You should seek to have credit cards that don't charge you for having it in your wallet! Why should you pay the credit card company for the privilege of them charging you interest? You're *already* paying them every time you use the card and keep a balance on it. Why pay more?

These are the thoughts and conversations we need to have before we apply for any new lines of credit. By maintaining a hyper-vigilance in regards to your credit report, you will begin to develop a sixth sense and will be able to almost intuitively ask the right questions to obtain the pieces of information you require in order to make an informed decision about applying, or not applying, for additional credit.

CHAPTER 5:
The Dreaded Topic: Collection Agencies!

Now THAT WE understand our credit report and have some strategies under our belt to manage our finances better we are now optimally situated to deal with the topic of collection agencies.

First, I will share the good news. There is a statute of limitation on debt meaning that after a very specific time period (based upon what state you live in) you will no longer be responsible for paying a debt after the statute of limitation has ended.

While I am not advocating that you do not pay your bills you should know what the statute of limitation is for your state. If you don't know please check out this chart to find out:

> *Bank Rate's State Statute of Limitations for Old Debts:*
> http://www.bankrate.com/finance/credit-cards/state-statutes-of-limitations-for-old-debts-1.aspx

Here's another piece of good news about bill collectors. In some states, the bill collector *must* tell you if the debt they are contacting you about has passed the statute of limitations. Somewhere in the letter they send you should be a paragraph that sounds something like this:

WE ARE REQUIRED BY LAW TO GIVE YOU THE FOLLOWING INFORMATION ABOUT THIS DEBT. The legal time limit (statute of limitations) for suing you to collect this debt has expired. However, if somebody sues you anyway to try to make you pay this debt, court rules REQUIRE YOU to tell the court that the statute of limitations has expired to prevent the creditor from obtaining a judgment. Even though the statute of limitations has expired, you may CHOOSE to make payments. However, BE AWARE: if you make a payment, the creditor's right to sue you to make you pay the entire debt may START AGAIN.

As you have just read, some other not so good news is if you happen to respond to a debt collector about a debt that has already gone past the statute of limitations you restart the clock for another cycle! They now can come after you for another however many years it is in your particular state.

This is where great organization, or research skills, come into play. If you have a credit card, or a cell phone bill, or a retail department store bill that you first incurred in 2005 in the state of Colorado by January 2012 that creditor will no longer be able to sue, or collect on this debt.

Here's some other not so great news. There are some creditors and collection agencies that are very shrewd. They will wait until a few months before the statute of limitations ends *and then sue you*. Yes, they take you to court four to six months before the bill goes out of their range which also happens to ruin your credit score.

Once a bill collector sues you (takes you to Civil Court for payment) the statute of limitation goes completely away. That bill and that particular bill collector can come after you for the rest of your life until you pay that debt. See, I told you this was not so good.

The worst part? Being taken to court is the *biggest most unpleasant* derogatory item that can be entered onto your credit report next to bankruptcy. If you are sued, this will go to all three credit reporting bureaus and that will stay there for 10 years. If the bureaus feel generous they can remove it after seven years but don't hold your breath.

If you are sued, this pops up *immediately* every time your credit report is pulled and you will be denied for *everything* you apply for — seriously, *everything*.

The only way around this is to go to court with all of your documentation and a very good reason why you did not pay the debt (lost job, divorce, pregnant/no job, etc.) and let the Judge know that you are back on your feet (or, not) and that you can pay X amount. Whatever amount you tell the judge you will be held to it. You *must* pay that amount when you say you will pay it.

Why? If you don't, now you've breached your agreement with Civil Court. This is a legal matter now, not just debt collection. Your creditor can now go back to court and tell the Judge you broke your agreement and the judge will allow that creditor to tack on all kinds of fees, penalties and *interest* usually retroactive to the beginning of this account going into collection. As you can imagine, this can be a pretty hefty sum. Just pay whatever it is you agreed upon in front of the Judge. In most cases, you can ask the Judge to pay as little as $20 - $75 per month on your debt. Yes! You can ask the Judge for the repayment amount you can easily afford. This is why going to court is the best thing you can do for yourself if you find yourself in this situation.

What if you can't afford to pay anything, you ask? Forget it. You have to be able to pay something even if it's $5.00 a month. You cannot walk into court and say you can't pay anything. The only way you can do that is if you are on medical leave/disability, you've sent a proxy to court for you and you have no other means of payment other than your disability check which is not enough to cover your everyday living costs. If that is your scenario, bring documentation to court to show your situation definitively. The more organized and prepared you are the better your argument will be to the Judge.

If you tracked every single payment you made to a creditor on the back of a napkin, or an envelope — bring that to the Judge! This way, the Judge can see that for X amount of years you tracked your payments — yes, in an unorthodox manner but you tracked it! This shows the judge you were, and still are, sincere in your desire to pay your debt.

If the Judge gets the sense that you are trying not to pay your bill things may not go so well for you.

Please do not ignore a summons to appear in Civil Court. Just. Don't. Do. It. I beg you…don't not go. Yeah, a double negative; love those, don't you? I hate double negatives but that is exactly where you are if you find yourself with a summons to appear in Civil Court and you don't go. You are effectively putting yourself in a double negative position. You can choose to make this right. Whatever it was that happened that opened the door for you to be here right now? It's done. It's over. That person is *no longer who you are*.

You can choose to take the high road and *choose* to be a new you for less than a $1 a day in many cases. Yes, for much less than a latte you can pay this bill and fix your credit right now. This is also an aspect of responsible financial stewardship because you are digging yourself and your family out of an undesirable past that you are choosing to step away from.

The moral of the collection story? Make payment arrangements at your earliest possible convenience when you know that it is your debt. This will save you tons of time and headaches down the road. Your credit score will thank you, also!

Here are some helpful links for your to start your own research on this hairy collection agency topic.

Federal Trade Commission:
https://www.consumer.ftc.gov/articles/0149-debt-collection

9 Secrets Your Deb Collector Does Not Want You to Know:
http://finance.yahoo.com/news/9-secrets-debt-collector-doesn-143024147.html

8 Things Debt Collectors Won't Tell You [Military.com]:
http://www.military.com/money/personal-finance/credit-debt-management/8-things-debt-collectors-wont-tell-you.html

Please note, this paragraph (page 30) was taken from a letter received by an acquaintance of the author.

CHAPTER 6:
The Solid Family Financial Stewardship Mindset

T HE RIGHT PLACE to begin this chapter is at the beginning. This beginning is where our collective financial woes commence and many things (usually all at once) go haywire. When is that moment? None other than when we decided *not* to track each and every penny that we spend each day.

Yes. You have to track what you spend. Do not try to censor your spending; just spend the way you normally would spend and keep track of it. At the end of the month — or, a 30-day time period so as not to wait to start at the beginning of the month if it's say, in the middle of the month, — tally up all the things you purchased into categories and then add it all up. Yes, you can do this via Quicken, Intuit, or any of those programs. You can even do this in Microsoft Excel. However, I prefer good 'ole paper and pen.

Now, that you have your totals, what are you spending the most money on? Does it surprise you? Were you aware you spent as much as you did in various categories? Or, how little when you thought you spent more?

I learned of the importance of this simple, yet powerful, tool when

I attended *Debtors Anonymous,* a 12-step group focused on assisting people who have debt and would like to overcome their dependence upon overspending. And no, I am *not* kidding.

Just the same way you can have an eating disorder you can have a spending disorder. I used to spend money to appease emotional wants and needs. If I didn't feel 100% on any given day, I would go out and buy myself something pretty to look at (jewelry, clothes, shoes, etc.), or give my money away to people who I thought were in need (totally another story!)

After I had children, many of these issues began correcting themselves as the money priorities had to change to accommodate the needs of the children. However, the roots of my money issues were still in place lying dormant. It was after my divorce that I realized the power of yoking into a group and sharing the energy of a common cause — learning to overcome negative money thought patterns and/ or letting money rule instead of using money to do what is needed and necessary.

Debtors Anonymous (DA) has chapters all across the country and they even have conference calls you can join if you cannot find a group in your local area. You can totally be a lurker in your first few meetings to get a sense of what is going on and listen to others. No matter your race, creed, beliefs, or sexual orientation money is always green and people can't get enough of it.

This 12-step program was extremely pivotal for me and allowed me to understand that money is an object that we can choose to use wisely, or allow it to rule our every waking moment.

As you progress through the 12 steps with DA, you learn how to get rid of financial ambiguity (*I'm not quite sure how much money I have in the bank. I don't really know the exact due date of my rent/ bills/utilities/etc. I have a pretty good idea when that letter came in from that collection agency; I put it in a safe place so I can really take a look at it when I have some time...*) by dealing with things head-on in a supportive group. You find people who can help you with what is basically an intervention to help you stop in your tracks and get a handle on your current finances. And all of this is *free.*

As with all 12-step programs, people give of their time and energy to help others succeed. Each one, teach one. There's a ton of literature that is very inexpensive and will help you to remember the things that have been identified in your support group that are very important for you to follow at this moment in your financial life.

Lastly, know that *everyone* is welcome in DA. If the first, third or ninth meeting you tried is not right — try another one, or go online for one of the conference call meetings. Do not allow anything, or anyone, to stop you from getting the most out of this wonderful group. The tools, the steps and the people in DA are sincere and quite passionate about helping others stay solvent one day at a time. You can find the link to the DA home page link in the appendix.

This short mention of DA is a big piece of the solid financial stewardship mindset. We cannot have a good relationship with money if we don't first understand how it works, how to manage it and how not to fear it. Yes! Fear is a definite component in why our money has not been working for us. We don't tend to use common sense when it comes to our money. We more flow with what is needed at the moment. Or, how we will be perceived by others (such as our children) if we do not give them what they want.

For those starting out in life and beginning the process of building credit, it is important to realize upfront that YOU are the one in control of your money. If you don't have a plan for your money when you get money in your grubby little hands *you will spend it* on whatever is in your mind. So, if that is the case, make sure that what is in your mind is the contents of your one-pager Master Finance sheet (make sure you download it!)

Use this sheet to help you say *NO!* to things that will lead you down the path of insolvency. What is insolvency? Using credit to buy things you cannot afford right now in this very moment.

DA advises that we try to go every day without using credit, meaning without going into debt. Using credit is going into debt. (The repetition is intentional!)

Once you understand and master the basics of finances, you can then use credit wisely but right now we are all taking baby steps to being awesome stewards of the family coffers.

Developing the habit of writing down everything you spend

coupled with not using your credit cards will help you to stick to what you have planned out in your one-pager Master Finances. Make sure you add in entertainment and/or a rewards category for yourself! For a job well done at financial stewardship you must give yourself a *gift* that you can easily afford.

My mother always told me that from every paycheck she bought herself something to reward herself for working so diligently to do what was best for us. She told me it didn't have to be much; it could have been an ice cream cone, an inexpensive item she saw and liked such as a silk scarf, or put down some money towards something that costs a bit more. Back then, there was this thing called "layaway." (What retailer does *that* anymore?)

"Layaway" is along the same lines of the easy-pays and flex-pays we talked about earlier. The only exception is that with the old-time layaway plans you did not get your item until you paid it off in full. The new version of this gives you *instant gratification* and allows you to have and enjoy your item as you're paying it off.

So, if you find a store that does layaway please don't ask them if you can take home your stuff after you make the first payment! They just may laugh at you. Simply go online and seek out reputable retailers that offer kinder, gentler payment terms which will stretch out payments and allow you to maintain your cash flow. I almost want to say it preserves your solvency but in the harsh light of reality you are going into debt with flex/easy-pays as it is a bill that will be billed to you for an additional two to four months.

However, you have done the work; you've created a Master Spending Plan. You are the only one that can say if easy/flex-pays are something you can indulge at this time in your financial life.

If you find you need to chat with someone about whether you should, or shouldn't indulge in these flexible payment plans you should talk to a trusted friend, or mentor. Or, you could leave me a comment on my website by clicking the tab with this book's name, or you can email me through the website.

CHAPTER 7:
Building & Maintaining Your Credit Profile Effectively...from Scratch

T HIS SECTION IS specifically for the college-age readers and even some high school seniors whose birthdays fall in late October, November and December (because you guys are typically older by one year due to the cutoff dates of the American public school system of when you can begin kindergarten and first-grade). This section would also be great for young adults starting out in life who have not yet made any steps towards creating a credit profile.

Hey Mom and Dad! Don't skip over this chapter as there are references to you here that you will need to know about and a few great tips to help you maintain your credit profile now and in the years to come.

I have had a profile with the credit reporting agencies for over 25 years now. That, in and of itself, is a helpful thing. However, if all of those years are not reporting positive, or even good, credit habits that long period of time then becomes a detriment.

Neophyte credit profiles you are at a pivotal point in your lives. You can begin making positive moves from the outset and lay the foundations for an obstacle-free credit life, or you can create a situation where you are working to come out from under the pall of credit missteps which you have read about up until this point. It's your choice.

By now, I'm sure you have so much information about *what not to do* that I almost only need to say do the opposite of everything you have read up until now. But, there is a bit more for you.

Option 1: Have your parents help you start/develop a credit profile.

This is a wise idea if your parents have a strong track record with the credit reporting agencies (read: a credit score of more than 680). Ask your parents for a meeting where you will discuss your financial future. Your goal for this meeting is to ask them to co-sign for a credit card for you.

What this means is the credit card will be approved on the strength of your parent's credit and the card will be in your name *but* if you fail to pay in a satisfactory manner your parents must pay on your behalf.

To this meeting bring your one-page Master Finance sheet, your spending over the past 30 – 60 days, and what your financial goals are for the next 12 months. This way, they know you're serious.

At the meeting, share all of this information with your parents and let them know what you're goals are and how you expect to make payments on the credit card you are asking them to co-sign on your behalf. Based upon your presentation and how you have dealt with money in the past few years, your parent(s) will either do it, or not. You will have a very good idea about if they will or won't if you're honest with yourself.

If they say yes, then you will have started a positive credit profile since your social security number will be attached to this account once it is opened. Once you have the card, make sure you know the due date, the interest rate, if there is an annual fee and how that fee is paid (monthly/yearly). You should also figure out what method you will use to pay this bill each and every month at least 2 ~3 days *before* the due date to ensure your payment is credited in a timely fashion.

Over time, if you handle this credit card well and you asked for this card prior to your 18th birthday, shortly after your 18th birthday this card will be shifted to your name alone and you will be solely responsible for it. Do check on this detail! Some institutions will do it automatically, others will require you, or your parent(s) to communicate with them about the removal of your parent(s) from the account.

Option 2: Applying for Credit on Your Own

As you near your 18th birthday, and in some cases, as early as your 16th birthday you will begin receiving credit card offers in the mail in your name. These will be pre-approved credit card offers with credit lines of $500 - $2,500. Yeah, you. The one without the job having a pre-approved credit card. Uh-huh.

As you can see, this is a very big set-up if you have had no training, or been given any information on how to manage such a very big responsibility. In this option, you kind of skipped over the financial meeting and received an offer of a credit card without the preparatory steps.

It is my most sage advice that you go back to option 1 read through and *do* all of the steps and *still speak to your parents* before you accept the credit card offer. Even if your parents do not have a credit score above 680, share this book with them and make sure you all have a very frank conversation about how this card can and will be used. Why? Because, even if you take the credit card offer, since you may not have a steady income your parent most probably will need to help you maintain this card successfully by helping you to make payments (and maybe even reminding you that the payment is due!) That adage about it takes a village to raise a child is true and with the prospect of developing good credit it is also true! It goes without saying that this new credit card is entered into your Master Finance sheet as soon as the card arrives along with all of the pertinent repayment details.

Obtaining credit at the beginning of your credit career is *easy-peasy*. To get additional credit offers (unless you receive and accept two or three offers, initially) will depend upon how you handle that first credit card.

If you do receive and accept two, or more, credit card offers initially, now the *real* work begins. You now must manage and maintain payment on your two+ credit cards. So, the work we detailed above about due dates, interest rates, annual fees and how those fees are paid is doubled, or tripled. You need to have these credit cards on your Master Finance sheet!

Due to you accepting either the one, or the several credit card offers your credit score will dip as you now have hard inquiries on your credit reports. Please note, not all of the credit reporting agencies will pick up all of the credit inquiries. Do not ask me why but all of your credit information does not *always* hit all three of your credit reports. In some wacko reality (that is the credit reporting agencies) a credit card, or two, may not be picked up by one of the three credit reporting agencies. This is where an annual check of your credit reports is key. You want to make sure that all of your credit information is reflected on all three credit reports: Equifax, Experian and Trans Union.

This step goes for *all readers*. Obtaining your annual credit report from www.annualcreditreports.com is very important! This is how you capture and contain fraudulent activity on your reports. You can ensure that all of your credit information has been reflected equally amongst the three credit bureaus. If your credit information is not uniform on all three then you send copies of the documents for the reporting bureau that is lacking and either upload the information to them online, or snail mail it to them.

If you're thinking, *Wow, managing and maintaining my credit profile is a full-time job!* You would be correct. It is. However, it is well worth it as a score above 680 will open many doors including renting an apartment in a safe, shop-filled neighborhood. It is also becoming more and more prevalent that potential employers are checking your credit before offering you employment. So, your credit score is becoming more and more important in our society — not less.

Now that you have a fab new credit card how will you pay your bill every month? Yep, you guessed it. You need a checking account at a bank. Today we have a plethora of choices for banking from the traditional brick and mortar banks —like Capital One, Emigrant Bank, Citibank, credit unions, etc. — to online banks (like ING, Ally and

PNC).

It is best to have a checking account that does not charge a fee if you have a direct deposit coming into it every month. Or, if you are not yet at the point where you have a regular income, make sure that the minimum amount you need to have in the account so you pay either nothing per month, or a very small fee, is something you can afford. There are a number of banks where the minimum you need to have in your checking account *every day* is $100, or less.

This is a very small price to pay when you consider having to pay a fee to a check cashing place each and every paycheck. Each time you use the check cashing place they charge you a fee depending upon the amount of the check you cash. When you add up all the check cashing fees at the end of the month it doesn't look like that much. Try adding that up by the end of the year — now you're talking about big bucks.

This goes for single moms and dads, too. Opening a checking account is an important building block in creating a solid financial base.

The next step is to have a savings account so you can *pay yourself first* when you get money — every time you get money! So, if you get a dollar, you should save 25 cents. The idea is that you are worth taking care of. By putting something away for yourself, you are ensuring that you have some money for that proverbial rainy day we're always hearing about.

Getting back to the credit card, you can use your checking account to pay your credit card bill automatically every month to ensure that you do not make a late payment. However, you must remember when the automatic debit comes out so that you can put the correct amount of money into your account *before* the debit comes out. This can be tricky especially if you have several automatic payments.

Until you get a nice rhythm going, you may want to manually pay your credit card bill(s), and other bills yourself. When you've got it down, then you can decide about going to automatic payments.

Now for the other scenario, if you don't have a checking account, you will have to go into the branch of the bank your credit card is issued from to make a payment. Or, you will have to send a money order — which costs money at most check cashing places — and buy a stamp each and every month to pay your bill. I don't know about you but I absolutely hate standing in line in the Post Office! Ultimately, it is up to you but I strongly suggest opening at least a checking account.

Here's a little anecdote shared with me by my good friend that will help emphasize the point of obtaining a checking account. Thanks Andrew!!

LA Times: Opinion — How Banking Works for People of No Account —
http://www.latimes.com/opinion/opinion-la/la-ol-bank-account-20150130-story.html

Next, I want to share Robert Kiyosaki's wonderful Cash Flow Classic game. You can play it online for *free*. This game teaches the young and old and everyone in between the basics of money. It can be a lot of fun when you play the board game but it is a bit pricey (usually well over $85 used; over $150 new). No matter how you play the "Rat Race" game you will learn something new about money and money management that you did not know previously.

Here is the link to the "Rat Race" game:
http://www.richdad.com/apps-games/cashflow-classic.aspx. Have fun playing!

If your interest is piqued here are a few oldies but goodies in terms of reading that I enjoyed and put to good use on how to manage and increase the greenbacks in your life. There are more and newer books available at your favorite bookstore, or online retailer by Suze Orman, T. Harv Eker, Dave Ramsey and Tony Robbins to name a few.

"Rich Dad, Poor Dad" *and* "Cash Flow Quadrant"
by Robert Kiyosaki

"The Wall Street Journal Guide to Understanding Personal Finance"
by Kenneth M. Morris & Alan M. Siegel

Kathy Kristof's "Complete Book of Dollars and Sense."

CHAPTER 8:
The Feel Good Part of Parenting

Now comes the "easy" part. Once you are on top of your monthly income and expenses using your Master Finances spreadsheet you can tackle the intangible stuff that kids also need. Like what? The questions on how to choose friends, how to stand one's ground without being nasty, or breaking your child's spirit, being able to set expectations and boundaries with friends. Oh, and my favorite: how to choose friends wisely.

Yeah, the "easy" part of parenting is the part that's next. What I discussed earlier in this short book is truly the simple nuts 'n bolts that help you have the headspace for the true meat of being a parent.

There is nothing I can say to you about these aspects as we are all individuals from different walks of life, different upbringings and different values. The priorities that I choose may be totally opposite of your values.

However, we do know that at the core of it, as parents, our personal relationship with money informs almost every single thing we do and affects our behavior, where and how we live. If you get the nuts 'n bolts down of being a great steward of the family's finances you can more easily handle the less tangible, more thorny topics of what to tell your fourth-grader daughter when she asks you to buy a miniskirt for her to wear to school...

I will leave you with a few more thoughts about things you already know.

SEEK OUT OTHER WAYS TO DISCIPLINE YOUR CHILD(REN) other than physical punishment. If a physical punishment is needed, in your opinion, in New York State you can discipline your child by hitting with your hand on the buttocks to the back of your child's thigh — that is it. In these days where raising your voice at your child can be considered abuse, parents — single mothers in particular — must be mindful. Please know that your child can call child protective services to report you. A perfect stranger can report you as well if they have first-hand knowledge of how you treat your child(ren). [Read: vengeful ex-spouses can have their current paramours call the authorities on you. Also, know that child care workers have seen and heard it all. They can identify true abuse when they see it. A word to the wise, do not coach your children on what to say; that will be ferreted out as well.]

Instead, think of punishments that impinge on your child's favorite things or activities. Take away that PlayStation, Xbox, or GameBoy. Limit TV, Internet, or other activities your child really enjoys. Instead of taking your child on a fun activity, leave the child home with family if they are not abiding by the ground rules you have laid out. Taking us to number 2.

LAY OUT GROUND RULES AHEAD OF TIME. DO NOT TELL THEM IN THE HEAT OF AN ARGUMENT WHAT YOU EXPECT OF THEM. See? You know this already. In essence, all of the things our parents did to us? Don't do it! [Sorry to all of the old school Moms out there!]

We are a different generation. We think differently from the way our parents thought. We have different options and opportunities — ones that our parents did not have. So, we need to do some things a bit differently than they did. One of those things is to give a basic list of expectations to our children either verbally, or written down. Both would be ideal. But, we are single parents. We do the best we can and we get better as we go along.

If we want them to do chores, have a chore list for each child. If you want them to have a certain grade point average in school, tell them what that is and what you will do if they achieve that score. If you want them to behave a certain way, or to cultivate a certain way of functioning help them understand why you want them to keep their room clean and why it is important. [*You'll be able to find your favorite baseball hat if you have one place that you put it when you come in.*]

DO NOT REWARD YOUR CHILD(REN) WITH TOYS AND THINGS THEY WANT IF THEY DO NOT ACHIEVE THE MINIMUM STANDARDS YOU'VE SET. OR, IF THEY DO NOT FOLLOW YOUR GROUND RULES. It's the same principle as when you're at work. Do you get a bonus or a raise when you don't perform your job well? Nope. Same rules should apply. This way, when your child goes out into the world they are not stunned.

Now, there is a school of thought that goes something like this: *Well, if I don't treat my child to the things he/ she wants they might go out and get it themselves.* That may be true but only if that is the way they've been trained. Or, if you are around others who have that belief and are sharing that belief with your child(ren).

STAY FIRM IN YOUR CHOICES AND THE REASONS YOU MADE THEM. DON'T LET OTHERS SHAKE YOUR RESOLVE. Part of rearing your child(ren) is to figure out who they are around. Sometimes, simply changing your environment can make a fundamental change in your child and how they behave. Hence, the reason why this book focuses on improving your financial life. Having resources, or access to resources through decent credit, gives you options that you may not have if you credit score is below 650.

Many times, the children of single parents do not feel they are given enough. They feel that they do not have as much as other children who have two parents. While in many cases this is true, simply because of the economics of the situation, by implementing the tips and suggestions above, your children will not feel that they are lacking anything. In fact, your kids may do more than those kids that *have* because you are more invested in giving your child the best.

Your parenting choices may make you unpopular among friends and family if they uphold ideals that you no longer choose to embody. However, you have to decide what is more important — you fitting in, or your children starting out life with more options than you did growing up.

My choices were not popular with my family but my eldest son now speaks Mandarin and spent a summer in China honing his skills. My middle son practiced gymnastics for 3 years and learned about self-discipline — a key skill young men need. My choices made me move from certain neighborhoods to reduce the threat of harm to my boys. My choices guided me to help my son write a story so he could see how much work went into writing a book. The result? He gained a grudging respect for books and began to read with more interest.

Yes, my choices were work-intensive but I am so glad I made the choices I did. This is partly why raising children is for the young!

CORRECT YOUR CHILD'S DICTION AND GRAMMAR EVERY SINGLE TIME THEY MAKE A FAUX PAS. This is one of the best and easiest ways to help your child's speaking abilities. [*Sweetie, it's not I axed for a chance to bat. It's I asked for a chance to bat.*] Yes, even little things like this should be corrected so that when they are not with you they (hopefully) will remember the correct way to pronounce certain words.

If you're not a hundred percent sure go online. There are a ton of programs that will sound out words for you so that you can give your children the right answers. In fact, send them to the Internet to answer their own questions. This way, they learn how to properly search the Internet to find answers.

Okay, I'm really done now. I hope something in these pages has helped you, or given you a different perspective that you feel will help you moving forward.

Happy Single Parenting! Remember, you are only one person. If you need help — ask for it. If you need to speak to someone else (like a talk therapist) that is OKAY...do it. It's better to vent to someone your own age who can handle it. And, they may give you some new thoughts and ideas to make your life better, *faster.*

CHAPTER 9:
Something Important for YOU

THERE IS ONE more thing that I have found is immeasurably valuable and that is *quiet* reflection time for yourself. Yes, this is totally an oxymoron. Which single parent has any time for themselves? But time we must FIND.

When you go and go and then go some more your emotional reserves wears thin and little things disturb your normally sanguine disposition. (Positivity rules!!) So, to head this crash off at the pass, if you find 20 – 50 minutes at least every other day (when the kids and significant other are asleep!!) you can use an app like Omvana, to find, download and listen to relaxing music with a guided meditation of your choosing attached.

It's important to have words and positive thoughts about the goals and things you want to work on pouring into your ears through your headphones just before you go to bed at night. Why? Because without additional effort on your part your subconscious mind takes in the new way of being that you are striving for and helps you to cut out the negative programming already in your head/mind/body/spirit from all of those years while growing up and living out there in the world soaking up everything that was ever said to you — the good, the bad and the indifferent.

To truly move forward, you must exorcise those negative and indifferent thoughts, one-by-one, so that you can move forward with your new thoughts with little to no hindrances.

You're unconsciously holding your own self back! In fact, there are whole groups of people out there in the world holding themselves back by clinging to societal negativity and baggage.

While you, personally, may not be consciously feeding in to the societal 'story' you may unconsciously have accepted it. Watch your actions carefully for the next few days and ask yourself what is *behind* those actions. The answers may pleasantly surprise you...or, they may not.

Either way, once you know what's going on under the radar, you can devise specific positive thought statements to help you combat the stuff you didn't even know was there. Or, enhance and build upon the good you've already uncovered!

Some great thoughts to consider...

I am, because I choose to be.

Happiness dwells within me every day, all day!

Forgetting all the slights sent my way is not necessary. Having forgiveness abundantly available in my heart *is* necessary.

Creating a life worth living is important and worth the effort!

Material wealth will enhance me because I now have emotional and physical health in abundance, as do all of the members of my family!

I am happy to be happy that I am happy!

Have fun in the process of creating your personalized positivity statements! They're for your eyes only. No one has to know. No one needs to see them. It's none of their business. This is all about you and what you need to move forward at this particular nanosecond.

Don't forget to check out apps such as Secret of Happiness. This app allows you to type up to 3 things that you are grateful for each day and one thing that you are happy about at the end of the day. This practice of expressing gratitude is very important in shifting your consciousness away from seeing lack/poverty/undesired actions everywhere.

No one is saying you shouldn't be a realist like Iggy Azalea. What I am saying is what we focus on tends to expand. You've lived your life the way you've lived your life for x amount of years, right? How has it been up until this point? If you're reading this book it may be possible that there is room for improvement in your current circumstance.

So, if your life hasn't been paved with blue diamonds and fabulous Alexandrite gemstones you could *try* it another way that doesn't cost you anything. Simply be grateful for all of the little teeny-weeny things.

Thank you, (your preferred name for the thing that you believe in that is bigger and greater than you) that the train came quickly.

Thank you, that the run in my stocking is underneath my skirt and no one can see it.

I am grateful for catching the chicken cacciatore before it burned.

Thank you, for that $3 win on the lotto today.

Thank you, for my co-worker acknowledging that I helped him/her today.

Thank you, for waking up this morning.
Thank you, for the world still being here and spinning as
it should under our collective feet today.

I am grateful that my health is good/doing better.

Thank you, for the laundry being done today.

Thank you, that the light, gas and rent are all paid on
time.

Thank you, that my rental/mortgage increase is
something I can afford.

Thank you, for the intelligence that guides me in my day-
to-day life.

Thank you, for my children!

I am grateful for the people who came before me in my
family/lineage/race because they did the best that they
could and now it's up to me to take it to the next level!

You get the idea. You can have little *Thank you* thoughts and you can have big *Thank you* thoughts. It's whatever you are feeling in that moment. Don't try and over think it — just go with it. Whatever comes out of your mouth/mind/spirit is what you need right now.

If you want more ideas from other people here are a multitude of quotes about gratitude posted on GoodReads — http://www. goodreads.com/quotes/tag/gratitude.

Another parting thought. Look out in the world, or at your family tree, and find someone you would like to use as a mentor model. Review their life/works and try to emulate their behavior and their example in your life, if possible. Or, just take the lessons they have shown and incorporate those lessons into your own life in the way that most works for you.

I love Maya Angelou. I cannot ever hope to be Maya but I can strive for excellence, honesty, and humbleness in every waking moment of my life.

Now, seriously, this is it. It's time to go out and try some of these tangible and intangible things so you can transform into the parent you've always dreamed and KNEW you could and can be.

Thank you for taking the time to read my perspective on being a single mom/parent. I have truly had a wonderful time sharing what has worked for me.

I wish you all a fabulously successful happy ride throughout the rest of your lives!

Acknowledgments

This book would not be complete without thanking some very important people — Sharon O. Tai, K.C. Wise and Andrew. Without the input of these very nurturing friends this book would not have been possible. I must also thank Karen, of KLM Editorial Services, for her undying support! Karen makes the words shine!

I would also like to thank my mother, Alma Campbell. She is a woman who taught me a great many things. She taught me how to say no. How to speak properly. How to understand the right way to move in a world filled with various colors of people. She taught me to stand up for myself and to know when to sit down and shut up. She taught me that loving myself, meant doing what was needed and necessary at that moment in time.

My Mom taught me so many things in the way she moved in the world. She's still here. Still moving. Still teaching. Thank you, Mom!

Appendix

• *Links to various state websites regarding their positions on payday loans*

Maryland:
http://www.onlinelendersalliance.org/news/137866/Maryland-goes-after-payday-lenders-banks-to-stop-illegal-loans.htm

Massachusetts:
http://www.mass.gov/ocabr/government/oca-agencies/dob-lp/consumer-advisiory-payday-loans-12232014.html

New Jersey:
http://www.state.nj.us/dobi/pressreleases/pr130408.html

Philadelphia (Federal Reserve Bank):
http://www.philadelphiafed.org/bank-resources/publications/compliance-corner/2002/first-quarter/q1cc1_02.cfm

Vermont:
http://www.cuna.org/Stay-Informed/News-Now/CU-System/Bergeron-on-hand-for-Vt--payday-lendersettlement/?CollectionId=8

• *Great information to use to defend yourself from predatory payday loan companies*

https://sites.google.com/site/paydaylenderssites/dealing-with-illegal-payday-lenders

http://forums.debtcc.com/paydayloan/dealingwith-illegallenders.html

• Free or Low-Cost Resources to Help Get You on the Right Financial Track

Debtors Anonymous: http://www.debtorsanonymous.org/

Federal Trade Commission ~ Coping with Debt: http://www.consumer.ftc.gov/articles/0150-coping-debt

National Foundation for Credit Counseling: https://www.nfcc.org/index.php

Credit Karma: https://creditkarma.com/

Department of Consumer Affairs Office of Financial Empowerment: http://www.nyc.gov/html/ofe/html/find/find.shtml

• Sites to help you with Positivity Thoughts & Reflection…

Omvana: http://www.omvana.com/

App: Secret of Happiness: https://play.google.com/store/apps/details?id=com.soh&hl=en

About the Author

Rochelle Campbell is a mother, a writer, an entrepreneur and a realist. With three kids spanning from a toddler to a 19-year-old, she has learned to figure things out on the fly. Creating solutions is one of the many hats she chooses to wear. Even when all plans don't work out the way she envisioned, Rochelle picks herself up and works out other ways to get things done. Her single mother motto is — *There's gotta be a way and I'm going to find it!*

Other Books by
ROCHELLE CAMPBELL

Leaping Out on Faith, a book of four short stories about women and the choices they make in tough situations - http://www.amazon.com/Leaping-Out-Faith-Rochelle-Campbell-ebook/dp/B007RGBQNA/

Fury From Hell (Book 1), a paranormal cop thriller, Detective Jennifer Holden has run from terrible things in her past that were beyond her control. As a homicide detective, there are some things Jennifer can't run from – her own demons and the demon that wants to possess her soul - **Soon to be released; check author page for more release date details!***

The Magic Seeds (softcover book for children), a modern-day fairy tale centering around the question of *What if we had a tree that grew precious gemstones...* - http://www.amazon.com/Magic-Seeds-Teraab-Ankhnu-Feaster/dp/1449007848/

Find and Follow
ROCHELLE CAMPBELL –

The NoteBook Blogairy Online

Twitter - @NoteBkBlogairy

GoodReads - http://www.goodreads.com/author/show/3434531.
Rochelle_Campbell

FaceBook - https://www.facebook.com/LeapingOutOnFaith and
https://www.facebook.com/RochelleScribe

LinkedIn - http://www.linkedin.com/pub/rochelle-campbell/14/
b83/248

Pinterest - http://www.pinterest.com/notebkblogairy/

Amazon Author Central (US): http://www.amazon.com/Rochelle-
Campbell/e/B007RHZNQ0/ref=ntt_dp_epwbk_0

Amazon Author Central (UK): http://www.amazon.co.uk/
Rochelle-Campbell/e/B007RHZNQ0/ref=ntt_dp_epwbk_0

www.ingramcontent.com/pod-product-compliance
Lightning Source LLC
Chambersburg PA
CBHW070940180526
45168CB00003B/1113